David's Little Town

A Memoir

Written by
David Scott Campbell

Edited by
Julian Costa

Library of Congress Cataloging-in-Publication Data:

Names:	Campbell, David Scott, 1941–2015, author
	Costa, Julian Thomas, 1989–, editor
Title:	David's Little Town
ISBN-13:	978-1-957863-17-7
BISAC:	BIO026000 BIOGRAPHY & AUTOBIOGRAPHY / Personal Memoirs

Disclaimer Statements:
Every attempt was made to preserve the style of the original manuscript. Only grammatical or mechanical changes were made.

The order of the stories has been changed for easier readership and to minimize redundancies.

Reprinted with permission of David Campbell's family.

Copyeditor/Proofreader:	Angel Ackerman
Layout Design:	Julian Costa
Design Assistance:	Gary Snyder
Printer and Binder:	Ingram Sparks

Photography credits: Gary Braman, Julian Costa, Michael D'Angelo. Additional photographs are from David Campbell's personal collection. All photos are used for editorial purposes only.

CONNECT with the publisher:

Substack:	parisianphoenixpublishing.substack.com
Web:	www.ParisianPhoenix.com
Facebook:	@parisianphoenixpublishing
Instagram:	@ parisianphoenix
LinkedIn:	@parisianphoenixpublishing
Patreon:	@parisianphoenix
TikTok:	@parisianphoenix
X (Twitter):	@parisbirdbooks

Published by Parisian Phoenix Publishing, Easton, Pennsylvania USA
Printed in the United States of America.

Table of Contents

Dedication

David Scott Campbell
September 23, 1941 – September 3, 2015

Introduction

Written by Julian Costa

David Campbell was an educator, television producer, and artist. He spent thirty-five years of his life teaching media and communication to learners young and old. His love for technology and creative expression flourished throughout his life, spanning photography, writing, and television production. But, beyond all of these interests, David Campbell traces his roots to the small town of Galion, Ohio.

During his retirement, Campbell set the goal for himself of writing a memoir. Within this manuscript, which he titled "I'm Just the Dad," he tells a vivid story of his upbringing, including the picturesque and the mundane. He reflected deeply on his youth and what life was like in that suburban town, sharing memories of grocery shopping with his parents, his first job, singing in the school chorus, and occasionally getting into trouble. Since only three copies of Campbell's memoir exist, very few have gotten to know Galion from his vantage point.

In the years since Campbell left "his little town," Galion has grown to a population of over ten thousand residents. It is home to over eight hundred businesses, ranging from manufacturing facilities to retail and grocery stores. The local newspaper, the *Galion Inquirer*, continues to circulate as it did during Campbell's childhood. The children of Galion continue to matriculate through the Galion City School

District, and families alike enjoy the Pickle Run Festival each July.

Memories of yesteryear are never far away in Galion, largely thanks to the dedicated work of the Galion Historical Society. One can find several landmarks within the town's seven-mile radius, such as the Adam Howard House, the Brownella Cottage, and the Hosford House, all of which date back to the 1800s. Though much of the industrial presence of the mid-twentieth century has disappeared, Galion maintains the qualities of a small American town that Campbell so fondly remembered.

My interest in Campbell's life came about when I was in college. I was working on a documentary project that traced my department's history, and through that project, got to know of Campbell and his many contributions as one of the department's founding faculty members. After he died, I felt as though his professional legacy deserved to live on, resulting in my writing of a biography, titled *David Campbell: Story of a Career* (2018). As I conducted the research for that biography, I came across many wonderful resources, one of which was Campbell's memoir. Because of the focus of the biography, many of the personal stories about his upbringing were not pertinent for that project but had so much value that they deserve to have broader distribution because of what they say about the town and the events that shaped the man I have grown to admire.

I had the joy of telling the story of Campbell's professional life as I saw it. Now, it is time for Campbell to bear the title of "author." This is his story, not mine.

Julian Costa
August, 2023

A Walk About Town

Galion, Ohio in the '40s and '50s had much the same effect on me as water has on fish. The area surrounds and affects, nurtures too, but for the most part, young people just swim along from day to day bumping into the glass enclosure, not really minding it or being aware of the water. And most days the water's the same, not too warm, seldom too cold. Of course, fish can't live out of water, so the analogy is not perfect. I left Galion's waters for good at 26, getting past the enclosures of a little town and while I have many fond memories, I am so much better having left.

My very first memory is of Mom pushing me the mile uptown in my stroller to Malloy's bakery where I would be given a sugar cookie. Malloy's was Galion's only bakery and while years later the large supermarkets would have their own in-store bakeries, theirs never came close to matching Malloy's with its brown waxed paper-wrapped loaves of white, bakery-fresh wheat and rye breads.

Malloy's bakery had two sizes of pies, a small, which must have been six inches across, and a full, closer to twelve. Cut into the top of a top crusted pie would be the letter of the variety, "A" for apple, "C" for cherry and "B" for blueberry. Their pies were a Saturday night treat in our home. I remember this not from my stroller years, but from my teens.

We lived in a nice two-bedroom house on a slightly oversized lot surrounded by fields on the north edge of town. The house was notable for its corner lot and the shutters beside all the downstairs windows. The backyard was large enough for an inning or two of softball or for afternoons of croquet. It was a three-block walk to North Elementary School, simply called "North" as in Galion the elementary schools then were North, South, East, and West.

"I went to North," I would say when meeting someone new to me. All the time I lived there, or stayed there, home for a visit from college, the back door was never locked, and our cars sat in the drive-way, keys in the ignition. Yes, burglars and car thieves existed then as now, we just felt secure.

My father, an electrical engineer at Galion's North Electric Manufacturing Company was kept from the draft of World War II, as his work there was deemed essential to the war effort. To help make ends meet, he worked some nights at Gledhill Manufacturing, building huge wooden crates to hold Gledhill road graders that were to be shipped overseas for use by the Army. Some of the 2 x 6's used for the crates made their way home one night and were assembled into a swing set that graced our back yard for many years.

Gardening

When I was very young, Dad had a garden on a lot he had purchased at the very end of the little street that ran beside us, Fortney Avenue. The cindered street ended and turned into a worn path as it passed the second and last house being ours. Dad owned the last lot, some six lots back. Our neighbor behind us, Dad's best friend, Gerald Bossler, owned the next to the last. Dad and Gerald tilled their plots by hand with a tiller/cultivator they stored above our garage.

My father raised many vegetables, the only crop I remember was popcorn. He would harvest it, then pack it in a large, netted bag to hang and dry on a water pipe in the basement ceiling near the furnace. Often on Saturday night we'd shell a cob and pop it, then listen to the living room radio. I can picture that large, standing, living room radio in my mind but there are no photographs. I can see in my mind: all of us listening to one of Harry Truman's campaign speeches in 1948 when someone in the audience shouted, "Give 'em hell, Harry!" And for some reason I recall two radio programs that we'd listen to together in the living room, "Henry Aldrich" and "Twenty Questions." Mom and Dad would drink beer and I'd get to finish the last mouthful or so from Dad's bottle.

Dad set aside about a square yard of dirt for me to garden. I planted radishes (which I didn't eat), carrots and leaf lettuce. Before long, my little patch would be overgrown. I had terrible hay fever* up until my thirties and being in grasses and the like resulted in terrific sneezing and watery eyes. My garden and gardening would be ignored once sneezing began. Actually, I was diagnosed as having hay fever at age one.

Dad and Gerald also raised chickens in an abandoned chicken coop across the side street. The coop and the cow barn beside it must have been used in the nineteen twenties. I can only remember once going along to purchase chicks, and experiencing one Saturday's chicken killing session. The de-feathered birds were stored in a freezer locker at a grocery store in the south part of town. I might have been four.

Dad and Gerald gave up chickens and gardening both shortly before my brother, Mike, was born when I was seven. The buildings were to be torn down and replaced by small homes. I think Dad's garden lot was sold for $600. A fine brick house now sits there. For many years the occupants had asparagus growing in their front yard, in what was Dad's garden.

---

* **Hay Fever** was a colloquial term for seasonal allergies usually associated with pollens

The Bakery

One of the best parts of Saturday when I was a boy in Ohio was the result of the phone call my mother made to the bakery placing her order. The best part of Saturday was when the bakery goods were unpacked in our kitchen. It was my father's habit to go to the office on Saturday mornings. He'd then stop at the bakery on his way home.

His noontime return to our house would be signaled by the Dodge's tires crunching the gravel in the driveway. Dad would come into the house carrying the bakery bag and the day's mail that he had picked up at the post office. The mail's contents held little interest to me. The bag's did. In the bag there would always be a loaf of what Mother and the bakery called "regular." Regular meant just a regular loaf of sliced white bread. To my palate there was nothing regular about it.

It was bakery bread, still warm and wrapped in a brown waxed paper with the ends neatly folded and heat-sealed. My mom and I both favored the heel, the last slice on each loaf's end that was basically all crust. There was a mixture and showiness about the heel when it was fresh and smoothed over with butter that was short lived.

Day-old bread didn't retain it and from experience we knew that the best time to eat the heel was then, while still warm. Sometimes

Mom and I would divide a heel. Other times we'd open both ends of the bread's wrapper so we both could have a whole end piece. The bread's waxed wrapper was never re-sealable but that mattered little in our eagerness.

While I checked on that delicious slice, I checked the bag's other contents. There would be another brown-waxed, paper-wrapped product: dinner rolls, either Parker House or clover leaf. They'd been Mom's selection to have with Saturday night's dinner. Her choice would always be what we had not had the preceding week. One Saturday would be Parker House, the next clover leaf and never the same to appear for two week's running.

Always, always on the bottom of the bag would be a small bakery pie. The bakery would have slipped it out of their pie pan into a heavy cardboard pan shaped to hold the pie's bottom intact. Over the top, to protect the pie, would be another white cardboard pan and the whole thing would be tied together with white string. I'd cut the string with a paring knife and lift the top cupboard to see what kind of pie we'd be having for dessert that night.

If the crust's center had a "C" indented that meant cherry. A "B" meant blueberry and pumpkin had no hiding top crust. Most times Dad and I would get a small piece to have after lunch and be instructed to save the rest for supper. Once my examination of the bag's contents finished, I'd put what wouldn't be used with lunch into the white metal bread box that sat on the kitchen's black linoleum countertop and prod Mom to get on with fixing lunch. I was hungry!

Childhood Ailments

I had what seems like more than my share of childhood illnesses: tonsillitis, chicken pox, measles, whooping cough and terrible headaches that caused me to repeatedly throw up. It wasn't until I was forty that those "sick headaches" were diagnosed by a neurologist as being migraines. My tonsils and adenoids were removed when I was six. This was a standard procedure for children then. Until my tonsils were removed, I would frequently be taken to Dr. Switzer's office and have my throat and tonsils sprayed with a number of medications, all of which tasted and smelled awful. The nurse's treat to me was as her last effort to spray my swollen lymphoid with air. That spraying produced no pain.

And it seemed that I was born flat footed and pigeon toed. I couldn't run without tripping over my feet. I wore shoe inserts and arch supports to turn my feet outward and to raise my aches until I was thirty.

I also endured eight years of orthodontia beginning in the fourth grade. My mouth was small. The teeth were coming in, crowning and pushing. My front teeth didn't meet. They were so crooked that I could not bite into a sandwich straight on but had to bite with my side teeth. Mom insisted that Dad take me to the town's only orthodontist.

This was in spite of the statement by our dentist who said that my teeth would straighten themselves.

Mom's concern was correct, and I went through braces, extractions, and head caps, which I wore at night and had metal wires and rubber bands pulling my teeth back on my jaw. There was great pain in some of that. Lots of tooth pain. Sometimes my teeth hurt so much that I could only eat Jello. However, I am eternally grateful that my parents pushed me through the process and that Dad could afford the bills. I wasn't finished with orthodontia until the eleventh grade.

In my little town, families went to the same dentist, a family dentist; the same physician, the family doctor; and men took their sons to their barber.

Our barber was "Drummy" or was simply called by his last name, "Drum." We had a fixed appointment, every other Saturday at 4. Today it seems odd that we went every two weeks. Nonetheless, guys did so then and Drummy was just as much a friend as our barber. Haircuts were a dollar until the late fifties when the price shot up to a dollar twenty-five.

The dentist and doctor were our friends, too. They knew us from our first childhood appointment through the time we went off to college.

Shopping

We had a neighborhood grocery store, the Summit Street Market, owned by the grandmotherly Bessie Barr. She wasn't always grandmotherly to kids though. If you dawdled too long in front of her glass candy case, "Well, wake up your mind!" would be her vocalized impatience. Mom would send me there for a loaf of Wonder bread, less than fifty cents, I think.

During summer afternoons my friends and I would head to the Summit Street Market for a bottle of Coke or an ice cream bar or a popsicle, then sit out front on the wooden bench that was built into the store's front. If we dripped ice cream or spilled our Coke, we heard about it from ole Bessie. Packs of chewing gum, Life Savers too were only a nickel.

A bottle of Coke was also five cents. If we took the bottle home, there was a two-cent deposit. A quart-sized bottle required a nickel deposit. Often, we'd raise money by cleaning out our family's garages of empty pop bottles and taking them in a wagon for cash, cash that would be used to buy treats.

One Halloween three or four of us set to wax Bessie's storefront windows from top to bottom. We walked right up to the store only to find Bessie and two of her friends sitting in wooden chairs staring right out at us. We always bypassed the Summit Street Market after that during Halloween time and were apprehensive about going in to buy anything after being almost caught in the act. Ole Bessie never said a thing to us about our dastardly plans, but I imagine she had a chuckle or two.

We bought most of my clothes at Penney's: Big Mac jeans, JCPenney underwear and socks, a pea coat for winter. That first Penney's, until it burned down in 1966, did not have cash registers at the checkouts. Instead, the clerk would write up the sale on his or her sales pad, take our cash and put it all into a metal pneumatic tube that was sent upward then across the store's ceiling to a location where the sales figures were double checked and then the sales slip and any change would be returned by tube in reverse.

Trains, Bikes, and Marbles

Like several of my friends, I had a train set, a Lionel that I received one Christmas. In succeeding Christmases for several years my uncle Fred would give me something to add to my layout: an additional car, a crossing gate, or the like. Eventually I bought a 4' x 8' quarter inch sheet of plywood and painted one side green, then added white roads. Atop the plywood I set up the tracks and the little pieces that went with it. Mine was not an elaborate set-up, and compared to today's video and computer games, was pretty pale. But it was a "guy" thing, boys had trains, set them up and watched them run round and round on their tracks.

As a boy, I had tired of walking and wanted a bike. "All the other kids have bikes," I'd plea. One of Mother's friends convinced her that I'd learn more easily on a girl's bike. I was completely against the idea. Yet the superintendent of schools delivered one night the yellow girl's bike that had made the rounds of several families to our home no less. He named the boys who had learned on it. Dad paid him ten dollars.

It seemed that I would never learn how to ride. I had little patience and great fear of falling. One spring evening Dad pushed me all the way up the little street beside our home and then proceeded to guide and push me back down. I was pedaling like crazy when I realized that Dad was no longer guiding me. I could ride a bike! I couldn't continue riding until the next day. Despite my success, I had a terrible headache (a migraine, I'd say now) and went right to bed.

For Christmas in the fourth grade, I got my first boy's bike, a maroon Schwinn. I heard a truck pull in the driveway late on Christmas Eve and peeked through my bedroom curtains to see the man across the street backing up his pickup. Carl was Galion's Studebaker dealer. His showroom was located near where Dad worked. On the truck bed was my bike! Dad had stored it at Carl's garage.

I tiptoed downstairs after everyone was asleep to see and touch the bike now in front of the Christmas tree. Uncle Fred was asleep on the couch. Daring and foolish, I pushed the bike's horn button. Luckily, the batteries hadn't been installed. That bike satisfied me until the eighth grade when I received a full-sized, two-speed Schwinn, green with white sidewalls no less. I rode it through the tenth grade.

In addition to "needing" and having bicycles, all boys needed marbles. We had two game versions. One called "snakes" where we knuckled our marbles after one another through the grass until we knuckled the other boy's marble and another version where a circle would be drawn on the blacktop or sidewalk and each boy would place a prized marble in the center. We'd take turns trying to knuckle the others' marbles from the circle and hopefully go home with more marbles than we arrived.

There were different classifications: steelies, which actually were steel ball bearings of various sizes and weights; pures which were prized marbles of a clear color; and cat eyes which were, as the name suggested, designed to look somewhat as a cat's eye. I was no great success at marbles but loved the sport. We would carry a few marbles to school in our jeans pocket in anticipation of a game during recess or to trade. My brother amassed hundreds of marbles, keeping them in a two-gallon New Era potato chip can in our bedroom.

Scouting

I spent three years in Cub Scouts, earning my wolf, bear and lion badges and the little arrow things that went on the breast pocket. Mother was a den mother for two years and I was in her den. That meant that I had to scrub the basement meeting place.

It also meant that Dad had to gather whatever materials Mom thought her Cubs should assemble or paint for their next project. We Cubs painted empty wooden nail barrels and assembled Styrofoam Christmas ornaments. There were birthday parties and games, too. From the mid-fifties on, Galion's Memorial Day parade went right by our house on its way to the cemetery. When I was in Cub Scouts and Boy Scouts, I was a parade marcher for that first holiday of summer.

It was in Boy Scouts that I was to receive the moniker that would follow me through school from the seventh grade on, and in somewhat limited ways now, "Bugs."

I was at the summer weeklong scout camp at Camp Avery Hand. The fellow who taught Morse Code with flag signals (I could never quite master Morse Code whether by flags or telegraph key) said, "I think I'll call you Bugs."

From then through my years of college, I was indeed known as "Bugs."

I loved Boy Scouts. It was fun. We met every Tuesday evening at 7 in the basement of the First Methodist Church. We were Galion's Troop 1. Many years later when troops were renumbered it became known as Galion's "Old Troop One." We, the members of that troop, always considered it to be the best one in town.

The knowledge and skills we were to amass in the process of earning merit badges and rank (Second Class, First Class, Life and Eagle) seem, in part, almost silly today. There was tree leaf identification, Morse Code, snakebite treatment, knot tying, marching in formation and the singing of scouting songs, loudly. All this was a small price to pay for what we really wanted to do — go camping.

I had slept out in my backyard in a tent Dad had bought from a colleague, first in blankets, then when I joined the scouts, in my Uncle Fred's World War II sleeping bag. But this paled against camping in a group of tents in a state park as a Scouting activity. We'd hike, go swimming, practice starting fires with a flint, stone and dry leaves.

And we were supposed to fix our own meals, storing the meats in ice chests and cooking atop a Coleman gas grill. I don't know that scouting builds men. I do know that it built great camaraderie and the few years that I was a Scout were good, filled with good times.

By the time I was in ninth grade, teachers called me "Bugs." There was a bit of notoriety in having such a nickname. I became better known, perhaps more popular.

There are people today, and all my high school classmates, that should I ever run into them or receive mail from them, I would naturally expect them to say, "Bugs!"

Summertime and Firecrackers

Before kids could drive, there was summer boredom to deal with, particularly before any of us had jobs. Oh, some guys had paper routes, delivering either the *Cleveland Plain Dealer* or the *Galion Inquirer* after school.

But other than riding our bikes, going for a swim in the park pool or at our doctor's home two blocks away, what was a kid in high school to do in the summer?

Well, some of us made firecrackers. One block down Market Street on opposite corners were two families each of which had two sons, bright sons. One father was an FBI agent. The other owned the town's largest construction company. Had their fathers known what we were up to…

Firecrackers were illegal in Ohio. One summer a foolish child had put a lit cherry bomb in his mouth, the story went, and the legislature banned both the sale and possession of anything that exploded.

In fact, my brother at 17 had a cherry bomb go off in his hand. The only way we had to obtain firecrackers was if we knew anyone who would be driving to Florida. Georgia then, just as Georgia now, was peppered with stores along the highway painted bright yellow with large red lettering announcing, "FIREWORKS!"

That summer after the tenth grade, none of us five boys knew of anyone who had gone that way, nor of anyone who possessed anything other than perhaps a few firecrackers that someone had graciously shared.

There was no Internet. There was, however, the Galion Public Library with its encyclopedias. We researched the ingredients for gunpowder: potassium nitrate, charcoal and sulfur. What we didn't find were the proportions.

Using these same ingredients, we tried many different combinations, test lighting each and filling our respective basements with smoke as we did. When we ran out of the components, drug stores filled our needs. We read elsewhere that potassium chlorate was even more powerful than nitrate. We also discovered that it needed to be crushed to a fine powder for faster ignition.

My combination produced a grayish blend. The other guys stuck with their black powder. We had one problem, actually a compound one, how to make a fuse and how to build a casing. After many tests and failures we somehow learned that the hardware store sold dynamite fuse. They sold dynamite, too, but we were not qualified to buy.

I discovered that those drawings I had produced in the drafting component of seventh and eighth grade industrial arts class were on a very heavy stock paper that could be cut, rolled, plugged with airplane cement on one end, stuffed with gunpowder then fitted with a three-inch length of dynamite fuse in the other. The making of the powder, cutting of the paper, and gluing were labors of love. With luck, the whole process was completed in an hour. We never built up a stockpile, preferring to fire our products that same day or night.

Yes, we could have been killed.

Television

Galion "BT" (Before Television) had two movie theaters, the Ohio and the State, both on Harding Way East. The Ohio showed a serial on Saturday nights. I cannot revive in my mind their plots, only that they would be in black and white and finish with some cliffhanger that often would bring Mom, Dad and me back the following Saturday night.

The first movie that I attended with friends and not my parents was *Bambi*. When I got home, Dad was washing his black '47 Dodge Coupe. I proceeded to tell him *Bambi*'s plot.

My telling, "It was in three parts," is still in my brain. The basis of the statement and whether or not I became teary at the killing are lost in me. I do remember the forest fire scene and how large and engulfing it had seemed on the Ohio movie theater screen.

In the fall of 1949, I became the first kid in school to have a television at home. I was in the third grade. When I went home for lunch there was a wooden crate that had been delivered by Railway Express and placed on the living room floor. Inside was a nine-inch Garod television set. Dad's friend at the telephone company in Lima, Ohio had found a place that sold them. I wanted it unpacked and operating immediately.

Well, that was impossible.

First, someone had to be found who could make an antenna. No stores were selling them. In the nearest town, Crestline, there was such a fellow. There was also someone at Galion's new TV store G & M. One of those stores delivered the antenna and Dad, with a fellow North engineer, got it onto the roof with a section of pipe, straps to tie it all to the chimney and dropped the antenna wire down the chimney as I sat in the living room watching for a television picture as they turned the antenna.

No clear picture was forthcoming. Additional gear was needed.

At that time, there were stations we could receive in Cleveland, Columbus and Toledo, Ohio, all at different compass points. Getting a "booster" to boost the television signal was only the first piece of additional gear. An antenna rotor was called for too.

Last was to be a 45-RPM record changer that would be placed atop the set. It had nothing to do with television, but the music that would be played through it would follow me all of my life.

TV programming was very limited at first, as was the proliferation of sets in Galion and towns across the country. There was no proliferation. When we'd take a ride in the car, we'd note the homes that had television antennas, a rarity.

I, of course, watched "Howdy Doody," Friday night boxing, dance programs that include camera shots of the spinning 45-RPM record and there was the video test pattern. Stations, lacking programming, would sign off around midnight but would leave a test pattern of circles in shades of black and gray on the air.

Dad spent many Sunday mornings with Mom's dresser mirror propped against a foot stool facing the screen while he tweaked adjustments from behind the set trying to get all those circles absolutely round and within the nine-inch screen. We had that set for many years before replacing it with a 21" Raytheon.

Then, on the last day of 1959, Dad bought an RCA color set. Dad packed the living room New Year's Day with neighbors to watch the Rose Bowl parade in fuzzy color. Only NBC broadcast in color and only one show a night. Thus, the program, whatever it might be, would be watched because it was in color. Somehow even commercials seemed better if they were in color.

As a boy, I watched things my friends would never. Having severe hay fever, I often stayed inside. I watched much of the Army-McCarthy Hearings, "Robert Montgomery Presents" and the political conventions. There was Lloyd Nolan's "Martin Kane, Private Eye," a detective show that I'd often watch alone on Fridays when Mom and Dad when out to eat at a nice restaurant. I sometimes hid behind a chair when a scene in the show would get too tense for me.

Family favorites were "Uncle Miltie," "Caesar's Hour" and "Fred Waring," and when I was in high school, "Maverick," "Perry Como," "Jackie Gleason," and "Bonanza." We almost always watched the "Huntley-Brinkley Report" on NBC, a fifteen-minute news program that came on at 6:30 followed by some sort of variety program, a different one each night.

Network news programs were only fifteen minutes until the 1960s. I watched the televised news coverage of *Brown v. The Board of Education**. It made little sense to me, as Galion was an all-white town. I assumed that Negroes had equal rights; knew little of segregation.

---

* **Brown v. The Board of Education of Topeka** was a 1954 landmark legal ruling that determined it was unconstitutional to segregate public schools based on race. This ruling was pivotal in starting the American Civil Rights Movement.

School Days at West and North

Kindergarten was at West school, a mile from home and a unique facility in that it housed grades K through 9. The high school's basketball team played there, Galion High's gym had no bleachers and was too small. Dad took me to afternoon kindergarten in his 1938 Dodge convertible, Ohio license plate BC-44. The 44 was just an easy to remember number.

My pleasure as a boy came not in riding with the top down but riding in the rumble seat that opened where there would have been a trunk on any other car. There was a rubber-topped step up on the left rear fender, a handle up top that turned and when pulled, opened a red-covered seat in the back of the Dodge. After one year at West, I attended North.

My elementary school, North, had but four rooms. Some grades were doubled up into one room. The two exceptions were the first and sixth grades. I vividly recall my first day in that old school.

Mom was ill. A neighbor walked me to first grade that morning. We had no idea which room housed the first grade. My teacher, Mrs. Stokley, was standing in the hall and spotted me. She was wearing a blue dress with silver apples. She had something in her ear. I had never before seen a hearing aid.

There was no gym. We didn't even have a gym teacher until I reached the third grade. There was, however, a music teacher who covered every grade at all four schools. She would go to the storage closet and bring out the triangle, tambourines, a drum and other child-sized instruments for the first graders to play. Also, there was a wind-up Victrola that had to be rolled from classroom to classroom.

Everyone walked to school, then home for lunch. There was no cafeteria. North truly was a neighborhood school. The farthest any kid would have lived would have been only five or six blocks. For me lunch was always the same: soup and sandwich with a glass of milk.

My acting debut came about in the first grade. Lacking a gym or auditorium, any performances whether they be choral or tableau had to take place in the classroom. The mothers were seated in the back of the room to see the performance staged up front before the chalkboard.

I was a bunny. I was embarrassed when while exiting the room at the play's end, the boy in front of me closed the classroom door and I was forced to drop character and stand in order to open the door. I'd been hopping up till that point, just as a bunny of course. Mother and her friends thought my exit was quite funny.

The New North School

In 1950, a new North School was completed, same name, new building. This one was closer, only two blocks from my home. By then, there were many homes on the street beside our house and two new streets beyond, all with homes and kids.

Children from the countryside were bussed to the new North School. One bus added those who lived at the Children's Home, a large brick residence for orphans on the western edge of town.

The music teachers now had an upright piano to roll from class-room to classroom. (All classes were on one floor.) We had a physical education teacher who met us in the gym/auditorium and taught us the bunny hop, square dancing and tumbling.

I was in different performances on that stage. In the fourth grade, I was a boy in *Tom Sawyer*, an all-school production. In the fifth, I played Eddie Cantor and sang "Ma, She's Making Eyes at Me" in the North Cub Scout pack minstrel show. My sixth grade performance had me as a boy who didn't want to go to school in some sort of patriotic tribute to the occasion of Ohio's sesquicentennial, "The Land Needs Book Learning."

In the sixth grade, I was the lieutenant in the North School safety patrol, the crossing guards. At each intersection up to two blocks from school in all directions were school patrol boys (I do not know why girls were not allowed) who were to secure the safe crossing of children going to and from school.

My being lieutenant meant that in case the captain of the school patrol was ever ill, I would make the rounds on my bike, intersection to intersection to check that all was well. I don't think the captain ever missed a day.

We were rotated intersection to intersection at the start of each month. My plumb location was right in front of our house. When I was on patrol there, my breakfast could be eaten at a more leisurely pace.

The new school had a blacktopped playground and spotlights that circled the building pointing outwards. These lights were turned on for evening events and to thwart the soaping of the school windows at Halloween.

Halloween

A week before Halloween, friends and I would pull ourselves up onto the roof of the school via the lightning rod cables and reach over the edge, carefully unscrewing each spot light just enough so that it would not light. This would allow us to perform any mischief, like soaping, that we had in mind.

There was a sense of community in my little town. School let out early one afternoon in late October so that kids could walk in the annual Halloween parade up Harding Way. Prizes were awarded for best costume and the like.

I either dressed as a cowboy or a bum. One year I donned a skeleton mask and walked as the "skeleton cowboy." I never won anything of course. That night there would be a parade with adults, bands and floats.

In preparation for these events, my friends and I would spend many days after school shelling corn that we had picked up in the cornfields not far from home. Those cobs, which the picker had dropped, were ours for the taking we figured. We'd each shell enough to fill a half a grocery bag. Our thumbs would get sore from pushing the hard kernels off the cobs. We would then lug our product up town then throw it at the floats in the parade and on front porches all the way home out North Market Street.

After School Socializing

For the most part, I really liked going to school, elementary, junior high and high school, too, not so much for the education but for the socialization. I rode my bike to school every day for the fourth through ninth grades. Then, my friends and I walked to high school until we had our own cars. Cool guys did not ride bikes to high school. They walked or drove a car.

After school let out in junior high, there were downtown destinations for many of us. The high school kids would go to Quay's drug store on the square. Quay's had a soda fountain with a black marble counter and swivel-back seats. Chuck Schultz's sister, Bobby Jane, worked the fountain, serving drinks, sandwiches and ice cream. When my bike would get a flat or broken chain, leaving me not enough time to walk home for lunch and return, I'd have lunch there.

The junior high kids would go to Tuttle's newsstand, also on the square, and belly up to the bar for a nickel Coke and a penny pretzel. Flavors for our Cokes added two cents to the tab.

Some days I'd go into Murphey's dime store and buy a quarter's worth of freshly roasted cashews, Mr. Peanut. Quay's had peanuts that were in a heated glass case, but they were brought in, not roasted in the store as the dime store ones were. The dime store air would be filled with a wonderful fragrance when peanuts were roasting in oil.

A really special treat was to arrive just as the nuts had finished being cooked: hot and fresh-roasted.

There was a period during high school years when many kids would gather at Isley's ice cream store with its soda fountain and booths. But most of us by the time, we were juniors or seniors who had a job after school at 4 o'clock and couldn't hang out at the ice cream place.

Going to the movies was a large part of our high school experience. Both the State and Ohio theaters closed following the opening of the Galion Theatre in 1952. Two sets of two double features, a newsreel and a cartoon would grace the Galion's screen each week.

One set of films would run Sunday through Wednesday, another Thursday through Saturday. We older kids would usually attend on Saturday night, first walking there, then riding our bikes until one of us at sixteen had access to a car.

A much younger crowd attended Saturday matinees. Popcorn was twenty-five cents; butter cup, a large cup of popcorn with actual heated butter dripped on top, thirty-five then fifty. I think that a child's admission was thirty-five cents. One dollar would cover admission and snacks unless we hungered for a butter cup, too. New ideas in filmmaking like 3D films seemed like big events then to kids and we would try to see each release. *The Wizard of Oz* was re-shown every summer and I never missed it.

Choir

I remember certain teachers of course, certain classes, too, but the significant years in school were the high school years. There was one commonality for me that began in junior high's seventh grade, and I experienced every year for six: choir.

My first organized singing experience was in church when I was in a junior choir. I liked that, and I liked learning the hymns. Many of the traditional Methodist hymns I know to this day, even though I haven't been a regular attendee in years.

I took chorus in school my last six years, sang in the ninth grade boys' ensemble, boys' glee club in the sophomore through senior years and the boys' quartet, "The Keynotes," my senior year. I could not read a note of music, nor play the scale on the piano, but loved singing with a group.

It was in my senior year that the quartet qualified to go to the Ohio finals in a singing competition which that year was held at Bowling Green State University. I had never before been on a college campus, something that my children regularly experienced beginning at age four. I would later choose to apply to BGSU. My only singing performance there as a college student would be in a summer theatre production of *Bye, Bye Birdie*.

Biology and Harold Friar

In trying to sort through the schooling mundane to give you some significant moments, I've culled my two best teachers, my first and second jobs and my first girlfriend. In my sophomore year there were a few academic choices: plain geometry or business math, Latin or Spanish, world history or biology. I chose geometry, a second year of Latin and biology.

Almost everyone took biology. There were five classes of it, one of world history. I didn't know why we all took biology., I simply went along with what nearly everyone else said they were choosing. To me at least, biology would seem to be more interesting than world history. In biology there were only enough texts to leave one in each desk (and not take it home), a broken microscope, no films, no slide series, but there was a chalkboard and the most energetic teacher I have ever encountered, Harold Friar.

Mr. Friar had been football coach a few years before, and he loved teaching, especially loved teaching biology. Using his enthusiasm and the chalkboard, he got us to discuss and to memorize all he possibly could cram into our biology class in the course of a school year. He'd pace, shout, point, and get us to repeat after him. In his own way, using himself as the sole resource, Mr. Friar got us interested, got us to memorize and got us to learn.

"Bugs!" he'd bellow. "Tell us why a cactus has needles and not leaves."

He became principal during my senior year and received a standing ovation at the first school assembly. I've never felt that administration was his forte. The first year that I taught in Galion he was still the high school principal. Back in 1958, administration was the only avenue for a schoolteacher who wanted to earn more. Harold had two sons, the oldest a genius, and he wanted them both to go onto college.

I did wish we could talk again, that I could share with him my teaching experiences. He died in 1993.

Speech and Miriam Sayre

Another career teacher, and Galion native, was Miriam Sayre who taught speech, dramatics and English lit. She was a Galion icon, known by all for her reputation as a teacher, play director, church organist and for keeping the same hairstyle for all her years.

She lived in what had been her parent's home, directly across the street from the high school's entrance. She never learned to drive until her fifties, preferring to take the train for long trips or to ride with her dear friend and fellow high school teacher Josephine Tracht who lived up the street. Her diction was as perfect as her posture. Her stories of Galion were a treasure to hear from her lips.

Her teaching was demanding in speech and English lit, relaxed and fun in dramatics. I loved it, loved her, loved her stories. I loved the scenes we'd have to act out in class and landed the lead in the spring play, What a Life! I had been smitten and bitten by the acting bug. I would choose to major in speech in college, get parts in a few productions and do summer stock in 1962.

I had attended plays at the high school, using the complimentary tickets that Dad, as a school board member, had been given, and thought I might like to be in a play, but was apprehensive about all of it, certainly about actually studying it.

I had signed up for speech class in my senior year. A week before school, Principal Friar called and said that I couldn't take both speech and choir as they were scheduled at the same time. I could, however, take dramatics, which met during second period. I did not want to give up choir and glee club, so I agreed.

Seated on my left in dramatics class was Peggy Schnelker. I first met her in the ninth grade. She'd attended the town's elementary parochial school (there was no Catholic high school in Galion), had an older sister who was a nun, another who had been homecoming queen our sophomore year, and an uncle who was a Giants linebacker. Our getting to know each other began in that class when I teased her that she was writing notes to a classmate, but never wrote one to me.

(I wonder if kids in school still write each other during the day or do they call each other on their cell phones during class changes?)

Anyway, soon we were not only writing notes to each other but I was driving her home at lunchtime, picking her up after. She thought I was the funniest guy and the best actor in the play.

We saw each other for six weeks before she told her mother that she could not decide between her previous boyfriend and me and wanted to ask us both to the senior prom. Peggy's mom had her stop dating all together. Peggy married the only guy she had gone "steady" with, Roger. Together, they quickly had five children. She died of cancer at thirty-four.

Censoring Books

It was in 1955 when I was in the eighth grade that Galion received national notoriety for something other than being a manufacturing town of road machinery and telephone equipment. My father had been elected to the Galion Board of Education, the School Board.

This five-member group was politically divided with two members, Dad and an attorney member supporting the superintendent of schools, while the other three members wanted their man in place. Time and again issues were resolved by a three/two vote.

The denouement came when one of the gang of three suggested that the monthly meeting take place in the high school library. As the board members walked by the stacks of books, one casually pulled one volume from the shelf, then two more.

He acted appalled that such books would be in the Galion High School library. This was followed by a three to two vote to close all the school libraries until it could be determined that all school library books were suitable for Galion's youth. The three books were Richard Wright's *The Native Son*, Hervey Allen's *Anthony Adverse* and *Toward the Morning*.

Galion's Catholic Priest was quoted as saying that all three were of "low moral level." One night during the next week, three reporters from *Life* magazine came to our home to interview Dad.

He was at work and Mom and I filled in. I told them how I'd been reading a book in study hall and had it taken from me by one of the student librarians. Every school library book was being called back. Mom tried to carefully present Dad's point of view regarding the issue.

When the reporters left, we hurried to look in our own bookcase to see if there were any books that might not be "suitable." Mom was convinced that the camera-carrying reporter who had stood by the bookcase, refusing a seat, had been photographing the Campbell family book collection with a hidden camera operated from his tie clip. In about three weeks' time someone from the state capitol or some place in authority told the Board to reopen the school libraries. Neither Mom nor our books ever graced *Life* magazine.

Teenager Antics

I did get in trouble in high school, once. It was the spring of my senior year. The chemistry/physics teacher was out and there was no substitute. Bored in physics class, some of us started tossing rubber stoppers at each other. I lobbed one at Tom who ducked and Karen took it on her glasses, shattering the left lens.

A hush fell over the classroom's lab. She was okay. I made my way to Principal Friar's office. He came storming in and told me that I had better leave. He had a friend in school that had lost an eye and this was not a time for rational discussion. I was to be in the principal's office first thing next morning.

The next morning, a calmer Harold Friar suspended me for three days. The next night was the spring choral concert. I had a solo.

"Not anymore you don't."

The night of the concert I slipped in the school and sat in the balcony. Unknown to me, Dad had managed to return from a business trip, arriving by train just in time to head for the high school and see his number one son perform. He went into the auditorium in the midst of the first number.

Harold spotted him and explained why his son was not on stage. When I got home there was Dad reading the paper.

The upside was that Karen was not blinded and that she, her mother and I became good friends. I was very lucky. So was she.

A First Job

My first honest-to-God job was at Weaver-Neffs' Supermarket, the newest grocery store in town and four blocks from our home. Friends had been hired there and I added my name to the store applicant list.

"I can't hire you, Dave, until you're sixteen," Bob Neff, the grocery store manager, had explained.

His brother, Bill, was a meat cutter. Parry Weaver was the third partner. He had hired both Neffs to work at his little store down Market Street a few years before. That store would deliver phone-ordered groceries to people's homes, including ours. Those orders for the Campbells always included a wooden case of soft drinks in bottles, usually Pepsi but sometimes 7-Up or Coke.

Shortly after I turned sixteen, Bob called, but only after Dad had reminded him that I was still interested and of age. I was to be a stocker and carry out. My pay was seventy-five cents an hour. After six months employment, there came a ten-cent an hour raise. All male employees were required to wear a white shirt, tie, and white apron. My only tie then was a clip-on bow tie. I possessed one white shirt. I was so skinny that the apron strings had to be wrapped around my waist before tying.

Stocking shelves was good work. I helped with the second aisle, the one with baking goods on one side, frozen food on the other. The store had only four aisles with a meat counter, then across the store's back.

Carrying out groceries was a pain. On Saturdays, bagging and carrying was all that was done by the stock boys. Often the work would be nonstop from the store's nine o'clock opening until whatever our sign out time was, either five or nine with hour breaks for lunch and dinner.

No tipping was expected except from the wives of two of the town's successful industrialist millionaires. We'd jostle each other at the three checkouts trying to be at the right spot when one of those ladies checked out and not be at another checker or out in the parking lot loading bags into someone's truck.

Usually these women would give a fifty-cent piece as their tip. Yes, wow!

The most I ever earned there was $1.25 an hour when one Sunday a month the floors would be stripped of wax and dirt then re-waxed. Store closing on Sunday was 2 p.m. and we'd turn off the front store lights, replace the dull 45's in the store's music system with rock and roll and start mopping and scrubbing. Four guys needed four hours to complete the task.

Driving

As teens, we were not unlike those portrayed in *American Graffiti* who drove back and forth, or cruised, on the downtown streets on warm summer nights, first in our father's car, then in our own. There was an A & W root beer drive-in on the west side of town, Porky's drive-in on the east. Each parking lot served as a turnaround point. I was the last in our group to get his driver's license. Success took four tries.

Testing took place at the driver's exam place in the county seat, Bucyrus. For my first test, I was fifteen minutes late and was not allowed to take either the written or the driving exam. My second attempt found me there on time where I quickly navigated the written exam, but failed piloting, both driving and the parking.

I had used my left foot on the brake, just as my father always had, causing the examiner to yell at me. Failing to parallel park into an imaginary space marked by four white flags followed this.

My third exam found me unable again to parallel park so that I had not located Dad's Buick within the minimum of six inches from the curb. In March, some six months after becoming sixteen, I finally passed the parking exam and received, at last, my license.

Gasoline was twenty-seven cents a gallon. Usually a dollar or two would cover a night's driving or "cruising" around while listening to the AM station out of Cleveland (KYW then). Another dollar would be needed for a burger, or a foot long, fries and Coke at Porky's.

A step up in cruising was to drive to the nearest town of any size, Mansfield, with its large downtown square and custom hot rods, driven by Fonzie-like* young men.

During our high school years we'd ride around in each other's cars, rarely leaving our little town for more than to see an out of town football or basketball game.

During our college summers when we could get a weekend away Jim, Larry, Keith and I often would head to Lake Erie, sleeping on the beach near Cedar Point in our Boy Scout sleeping bags or near Indian Lake, an amusement park south of Lima. There we'd find a place in the country to sleep, some in the car, some on the ground. I'd awaken with sinuses plugged solid and a headache from all the beer consumed the night before.

In August 1961, Jim and I took Dad's 1960 blue Chevy Impala convertible and drove to Yellowstone to see Keith who had taken a summer job before. Jim and I slept under the stars until we got to Yellowstone then pitched a tent in a campground not far from the Yellowstone Lodge.

---

*   **"Fonzie-like"** refers to Arthur "Fonzie" Fonzarelli from the ABC television sitcom "Happy Days," which depicted suburban life in the 1950s.

Prom and Graduation

My closest friends through high school were Cluck Schultz, whose choice to apply to Bowling Green State University influenced me; Jim Blosser, the superintendent's son, whose later choice of IU for grad school helped me pick the same; Larry Miley and Keith Baker, both of whom went to Ohio State and Everett Resh who went to a business school in Columbus.

All of us had nicknames: Chuck was "Schultzie," Jim was "Bean Blossom" or just "Bean," Larry Miley was "Smile-O," Keith Baker was known only as "Bake" and most kids called Everett "Moo" (as he was as big as a cow).

Of this mix, only Jim dated much, was the only one who had gone "steady," and he had the coolest cars. His red '49 Olds fastback was followed by a '54 Ford convertible. Bake, Ev and I all decorated our cars. Ev's "flamed" Buick was an eye catcher for its size and flames and for its shot shocks. When he drove across Galion's many sets of railroad tracks, he had to proceed slowly, or he'd scrape bottom.

Ev's parents, Frake and Bernadette, owned Resh's Take Away on Harding Way East, a place for beer, pop (In Ohio we never called soft drinks "soda") and cold cuts. Keith's father worked with Dad at North. They were in a group of four engineers who spent six weeks in Sweden in 1955 studying production techniques. Larry's dad worked at the Galion Iron Works and Schultzie's father was a salesman for an office supply company.

I didn't have a date for the prom. The only time that I had dated during high school was for a six-week period during my senior year. She had made her prom plans before we became an item. When we no longer went out together, she slipped back to the guy before me. There would have been a problem should we have gone to the prom together: I didn't know beans about dancing.

There were six of us (guys) without dates who nonetheless went to the prom. (The prom was at the junior high, the high school's gym was too small.) We all had cars, but I don't recall where we parked them all. What we lacked of fortitude in getting dates was surpassed in our ability to put together thirst-quenching refreshments: a case of beer, a fifth of Scotch, and a bottle of sweet vermouth. The one of us whose parents owned a carry out supplied the beer and vermouth. The Scotch was supplied by a friend who had a twenty-one-year-old friend who would go to the liquor store for him.

Not to be outdone, I supplied a four-pound skyrocket. (Where it came from is a whole other story.) You never knew when you might want to light up the sky with a four-pound skyrocket!

We went to the dance and from time to time left the dance to indulge in thirst relief. One of us favored the Scotch. One sip told me that it would not be my drink of choice.

When the prom ended there were other places to go. The parents had rented both the bowling alley and the movie house for our entertainment. We'd had too much beer to bowl, so we visited the theater. The one of us which had taken on the Scotch as his drink (with a few brews in between hits to the bottle) proceeded to throw up a river of the most foul-smelling vomit. We got him to his car where he was supposed to sober up by sleeping in the back seat.

The rest of us proceeded to head for Lake Erie. I don't remember exactly why. Maybe we were going to Cedar Point. We pulled into Sandusky about midnight and stopped at a shopping venter's parking lot to relieve ourselves.

The one who was driving burned rubber leaving and we were soon having a red light flashing behind us. The cop was curious as to why we'd pulled out of the shopping center with such speed. He asked to see the inside of the trunk. We were too young to buy liquor so he surmised that we must have stolen it from a store in a shopping center. We were to follow him to the police station.

Once inside, he discovered that we were reluctant to discuss the whereabouts of our liquor procurement. He proceeded to interrogate us singularly. I was first. He took me into a room with a long table and sat opposite me.

"Where did you guys get the booze?" he asked.

I replied that I didn't have to tell him anything, that this was not a court of law. (I was trying to protect the one of us who had taken the beer from his parents' store.) He blew up.

"What's a matter with you kid? Been watching too much TV?! Reading too many comic books?! Come with me!"

He led me to the jail cell, pushed me inside and as he slammed the steel door asked, "How do you like that?"

He then proceeded to question the next one of us by stating that I was already locked up, how would he like to be, too? My friend, the one who had taken from his parents, proceeded to tell all.

I was in turn let out and we were sent out of town and told to check in with the Galion Police Force when we got back to our hometown. We never did get to see Cedar Point.

The next day, Saturday, I met my dad as he was looking through the mail with, "I got thrown in jail last night."

"You probably deserved it," he knowingly replied.

The last week of school my senior year consisted of a series of parties, rehearsals for Baccalaureate and Commencement and the actual night of graduation, Friday May 29, 1959. We were excused from classes. Baccalaureate was a Sunday night religious ceremony held at the stadium. The songs were sentimental, religious too. We marched in our caps and gowns across the field towards the bleachers where our parents sat.

Commencement was to be outdoors also but it rained that following Friday and we had to sit on the stage of the not air conditioned auditorium and listen to a most long-winded address by a college professor.

Afterwards Keith, Larry and I gathered at the garage where an acquaintance made stock cards. We shared a warm beer. Peggy Lee summed it up so well with her song, "Is that all there is?"

I had no inkling that in six years I would return to Galion High as a teacher.

A Second Job

After graduating from high school, I was hired by our family doctor and his wife to assist their groundskeeper on their thirteen-acre estate. The pay was one dollar an hour with no withholdings. The Switzers owned a stately home with a long expanse of front lawn two blocks out North Market Street past our house. (Their daughter Marty and I had been classmates beginning with the first grade.) The thirteen-acre property covered almost two city blocks.

Behind their home was what was reported to be the largest private swimming pool in Ohio; a pony shed for when their kids owned a pony, which was then used to store the tractor and lawn equipment; a clay tennis court and a clubhouse near the pool's shallow end.

I mowed, weeded, mulched, painted and swam. For the first time in my life I got tan, as I could not be staying inside when hay fever season arrived.

I also freely borrowed their '59 Cadillac or '58 Lincoln, leaving my Bugs-decorated Chevy parked near their garage. This enjoyable job was to be my last employment until my fourth year at Bowling Green State University when I was hired to work in their television studio.

Small Town Life

My little town, as towns across America then, operated differently than today. Shops closed on Wednesday afternoons. This included barbers and the banks. Downtown businesses would be open on Saturday evenings, not Friday night, though I do remember when shopping in downtown Galion on Saturday nights was dropped and stores changed to Friday. On Good Friday nearly every store closed. The assumption was that people would go to church. And the national holidays of Memorial Day and Labor Days were not shopping days. Stores closed. Time was to be spent at home with the family.

As a boy, I often went with Dad to Galion's high school football games. I only went for the hot dogs. The half-time special performance called for the football field's lights to be turned off while the band marched, a small amber penlight on each band member's cap glowing on the field. The audience would "ohh" and "ahh" at the sight. For unknown reasons the practice was dropped by the time I attended high school and was cooking the hot dogs in the Hi-Y concession stand for Galion High's football games.

It seemed at times that everyone in Galion knew Dad. That wasn't true of course, but he was well known. Two organizations were dear to him, the Kiwanis and the annual "Cotton Pickers Minstrel."

Kiwanis then was an all-men organization that met for lunch every Tuesday at Galion's Hotel Talbot on the square. These were social gatherings that would be followed by a speech or presentation of some sort. Four times I was the guest.

Once as a third grade Cub scout, reading an article from a magazine Dad had asked me to read, once as a Boy Scout along with several others to talk about scouting, twice as a high school senior. As a senior I gave a reading of a humorous piece by Robert Benchley then at another time sang with the boys' quartet.

There also was an annual Kiwanis Day peanut sale. Small bags of salted peanuts in the shell would be sold at a Friday football game, then all day (until there were no more) Saturday on the town's main street. Price: fifteen cents. There were a couple of years that I helped.

School kids went door to door sold tickets for the minstrels. I was one who sold quite a few in the fourth, fifth and sixth grades, receiving a prize for my efforts in the fifth grade. I got to go to the North School PTA meeting, be introduced and received a silver dollar and a thank you from the principal.

A big event in my little town was the annual fall festival that the elementary schools held in their cafeterias and gymnasiums. This was a money-raising event, a true family affair for the kids of that school and their parents. The cafeteria dinner consisted of hot dogs or chicken sandwiches and lots of salad and dessert choices. There would be games of chance in the gym, movies in one of the classrooms, helium-filled balloons, handmade items for sale and square dancing. People from all over town would attend, not just those close to a particular school.

Galion had a population of 10,000, maybe 12,000 by the time I graduated from college. It was a manufacturing center of some significance with the Galion Iron Works, the world's largest manufacturer of road machinery; Perfection, a major manufacturer of dump trucks; two grave vault companies; and the North Electric Manufacturing Company, which was called "North" by everyone.

The town was served by two railroads, the New York Central and the Erie. Trains crossed through town every day and night carrying freight, mail, and passengers. The New York Central had a switching yard about two miles east of our house.

I remember lying awake on summer nights in the fifties, hearing the diesel switch engines push the freight cars back and forth onto different tracks to make up changed freight car combinations which would leave later. It was a very pleasant sound.

The Erie Railroad crossed the south part of town, right beside where Dad worked and the Pennsylvania, called the "Pensy," went through Galion's closest town, Crestline. Train travel to all parts of the country was reasonably close.

Living where we did out on North Market Street, away from all sizable highways, sounds were few at night and carried for miles. I would easily recognize the sound of Doc Switzer's Cadillac as he passed our house going home after late hospital rounds. We kids knew the unique sound of everyone's car who lived on our side street.

There was the sound of the milk truck, its empty bottles rattling within that is no longer heard today. We, as did most neighbors, had home delivery of milk three mornings a week.

But the most unique sound in our neighborhood came from two houses up Market Street, from Mrs. Newman, dubbed "Old Lady Newman," who would step out her back door some summer nights and cuss out the neighbors at full volume. She was a recluse, the story goes, who had some years earlier "flipped" and tossed all of her husband's clothes out onto the yard. He left.

A nephew would come with groceries and to mow her grass but no one else ever visited. She rarely was seen away from her home, had no car, no friends. She had psychological problems that caused her to react to annoyances by standing outside and shouting in the most colorful way and only on a warm summer's night. Her carryings on were harmless, albeit annoying to some, humorous, too.

She was intelligent enough to spot a patrol car approaching and cease her ranting. A well-meaning and fed-up neighbor set her up by having the chief of police at his home one night and then repeatedly flicked on and off his porch lights. Newman raised a ruckus and was institutionalized. After returning home she was heard again, but rarely.

Once each summer, unique advertising would appear in Galion. A single engine plane would be heard buzzing back and forth overhead. Kids, then their moms, would be drawn outside to look up and see what was going on — skywriting.

The pilot would execute with amazing precision the Coca Cola or some other soft drink logo in white smoke behind his plane. This was an amazing sight to watch. It was short lived. The smoke would dissipate and only the sky and the viewer's memory of what had been drawn would remain.

Almost Forty Years Later

In August, 1994, I went to my high school reunion, my first such return in the eighteen years since Mom had died, thirty-five years since my graduation.

Galion is still Galion, sort of a nondescript middle American town that's pretty much asleep these days. The hotel's boarded up. Penney's is gone…

Good grief! They painted the water tower orange and blue! It's a faded school color combination now, even sadder.

Out on Market Street, past 697, I headed to Neffs' to get the potato chips that aren't available anywhere but mid and north-central Ohio. I bought a four-pack box.

The checker said, "Either you're having a picnic or from out of town."

I did note that the original section of the store retains its green and white floor tile that I used to scrub and mop in 1958.

The cemetery looked very peaceful, really nicely landscaped and freshly mowed. I walked all the rows in the unraised marker section of Mom's and Dad's ticked that the stones don't all go in the same direction and the walkways are too narrow. Jessie Pickering has died but her husband lives on at 94 according to the stone. I visited Jean Switzer's then left slowly.

I do not know if I'll ever be back. It was my first visit since Mom was interred in 1976.

I had to visit our old house. The lady I met there, baby on arm with dog yapping at her feet, seemed pleased with the place. After a few awkward attempts to get conversation going, she let me into the home.

I wasn't bothered by what I saw. Change does take place. Their furniture, all overstuffed, was pulled out from the walls and the place was littered with kid's stuff. They have put in a patio in back, ripped out the bushes that I had planted, and plan to put a bedroom over our family room, tear down the garage and build a new one. Adieu.

As one o'clock approached, there really was nothing else left to do but head to the country club where the class of 1959 was to gather around the pool and reminisce until dinnertime at 6 p.m.

Oh, I did travel up and down the streets of my little town but nothing really noteworthy caught my eye. Around 5 p.m., I got dressed and rested in the car until people started to go into the club about 6 p.m. I joined two guys at the bar that I still don't know who they were and waited.

Probably the most fun was just sorta staring at old friends and letting them figure out who the hell I was. Smile-O and Bake reacted identically.

They stared for what seemed a long time then asked, "Bugs?" When I acknowledged, each exclaimed, "You son of a bitch!" It was fun. There was electricity in the air.

I ate with Bake and Smile-O at a table with George Zachman and his wife. A lot of people were on my case because neither Schultzie nor Blosser were there. I don't remember squat about Zachman, and his wife kept staring with open-mouth amazement at Smile-O and Bake and I as we regaled our high school and college exploits. Finally, I asked her forgiveness, explaining that we hadn't seen each other for some time.

About midnight I told Bake and Smile-O that I had to go. Bake said, "Hey, we gotta do this again sometime!"

I visited my little town again in August, 2000. I wanted to see it once more before moving to Naples, Florida. Visiting was both nostalgic and sad.

The Galion Iron Works, the world's largest manufacturer of road machinery, and the North Electric, for years a leading manufacturer of telephones and switchboards, are both shut down.

That street that we cruised, Harding Way, Galion's "Main Street," has only the corner drug store and the Elks Club remaining from my youth. There are no clothing or shoe stores, no newsstands either. Many storefronts are empty. The Galion theater shows no films, has been a restaurant and now houses a flea market.

I went by North School that day, as I wanted to see if my initials had stood the test of time. When the swing sets had been put in fresh concrete supports in 1950, I put my initials into one spot of concrete before it hardened. Gone. There is no playground equipment there anymore. Even in the town's park the swing sets have no swings and the slides are gone.

There were priorities for that visit. One was getting the famous and delicious Ballreich potato chips from Neffs', where I'd carried out groceries my high school senior year. The parking lot is potholed. The store's ceiling shows leaks.

But there they were, Ballreich's, and I got four pounds of them.

"You must really like those chips," the checker quipped.

The cemetery seemed different. Some of the maple trees that shaded near where my parents are interred are gone. I stood silent.

What can one do or say standing over his parents' gravestone?

I pressed my fingers to my lips, then to the stone and set to pulling back some grass and weeds. I stayed for a while, looking for the stones of others I might have known, particularly my first girlfriend, found Schultzie's parents' marker, then headed, perhaps one last time, to see the house on North Market Street. I was surprised.

There's a two-story addition where the garage was with a two-car garage behind it, new siding, a brick front walk and some strange banners on the front door and beside it. Actually it looks quite nice, just so different.

Galion's downtown hotel is condemned, its sidewalk blocked to protect passers by from falling bricks.

I wanted to go in the church where I'd been baptized and where Dad's funeral had been held. It was locked. I photographed the downtown, then left.

I still consider Galion to be my little town and I enjoyed living there and treasure the friendships and the times spent in our family home. I could not imagine being raised anywhere else or by anyone else. Everyone else's parents paled in comparison to mine I believed.

Keith Baker said it best when in the eleventh grade he exclaimed, "Bugs, your dad's the best!"

When I went away to college, I could not wait to get home, see friends, sleep in my own bed, cook and eat in our kitchen, shop at the store where I had worked. Life was good in that little town.

David Campbell

David Campbell's original memoir, completed in 2001.

About David Campbell

D avid Scott Campbell was born on September 23, 1941, in Galion, Ohio. As a child, he was an active volunteer in the community and worked hard to help charitable organizations. He also participated in dramatics and musical groups throughout his years of schooling. Upon graduating from Galion High School in 1959, Campbell attended Bowling Green State University, where he majored in Speech and English while earning a secondary education teacher credential.

Campbell began his teaching career in 1964 at Linden-McKinley High School in Columbus, prior to returning to his hometown to teach at Galion High School for two years. Campbell then pursued a master's degree in Audio Visual Communications at Indiana University, Bloomington, graduating in 1968. Later that year, Campbell was hired into the newly-established Communication Division at Clarion State College in Clarion, Pennsylvania.

In 1970, East Stroudsburg State College in Pennsylvania hired Campbell to help develop a communication teacher certification degree program as well as establish the first color television studio in the PA State College System. Throughout his thirty-year tenure at East Stroudsburg, Campbell taught courses in television production, photography, instructional media, computer skills, and multi-image presentation design. His students used their technical skills to contribute to community organizations, raise money for the local hospital, and gain real-world experience in media production.

Upon retiring from teaching in 2000, Campbell moved to Naples, Florida, where he volunteered his photography skills at the local animal shelter in order to help orphan pets find homes. He enjoyed traveling and taking pictures of his findings across the globe. Most importantly, he enjoyed spending time with his three children.

David Campbell passed away on September 3, 2015, at the age of seventy-three. His ashes were spread across Lake Erie.

Excerpt

David Campbell: Story of a Career

Written by Julian Costa

How does one decide upon a career path? It could it be the result of diligent planning. It could also come from the examples set by parents and relatives, stemming from a family legacy within a particular vocation. In some cases, our life's direction comes from the culmination of many interests, dreams, and ideas starting to take flight in an arrangement that one had never before considered, a result of circumstance, or simply being in the right (or wrong) place at the right time. It is safe to assume that when Robert and MaryJane Campbell were blessed with their first-born son, David, they did not know what career path he would take, nor did they expect him to pursue a career in higher education. When telling the story of a life, it is neither practical nor realistic to begin at the person's birth. However, in many ways, happily or disgracefully, we are a product of where we come from. Let us begin where the story truly started, about one hundred miles south of Cleveland, and nearly 140 miles east of Columbus, in the small town of Kilgore, Ohio.

It was to the small town of Kilgore, consisting of farmland, churches, and feed stores, that Jesse (Mc)Campbell emigrated from Scotland in 1747. Eventually, the family established a farm in Kilgore that they would own until 1975. Since this book is not a genealogy, let us skip ahead to the more relevant facets of the family history.

On November 7, 1885, Jesse Orin Campbell was born. Jesse, also known as "J.O.," grew up on Campbell Farm in Kilgore. He never graduated high school but instead took a correspondence course on telephony, which was a relatively young field. Only nine years before his birth speech educator Alexander Graham Bell patented the telephone. By investing time and effort into mastering this cutting-edge technology, he went on to build a flourishing career in telecommunication. His obituary, for which a date and publication title could not be found, compliments his work.

> Displaying early in his career pronounced managerial ability and a capacity for hard work, Mr. Campbell made a splen did record as an executive and much of the success of the great Ohio Northern Telephone Co., which is the largest independent corporation of its kind in Ohio, may be attributed to him.

J.O.'s work eventually took him from Kilgore to a town in northern Ohio called Norwalk. Here he spent twenty-four years at the telephone company but also gained local fame for his technological prowess. After visiting a convention in Chicago and being one of the first to own a radio in Norwalk, he got the idea to develop the "radiophone." The device, which utilized wet-cell batteries, was situated in the Campbell home and included a speaker with an on/off knob. Through a series of wires, the device in their home was connected to the telephone company where the signal was amplified. Many homes and businesses throughout Norwalk and surrounding towns paid monthly fees to have speakers installed in their homes. Essentially, the device provided a radio signal via telephone lines. Consequently, J.O. served as not only the engineer of this setup but Norwalk's first DJ, as he selected the station to be broadcast each day.

Though work was important to J.O., so was his community. He was active in community organizations, including his church, the Kiwanis club, and others. His obituary says, "[H]e displayed consistently a fine spirit of courtesy and consideration of others that won for him the respect and esteem of a remarkably wide circle of friends."

Beyond all of these activities, J.O. was a father, and like many caring parents, he involved his children in his professional and social activities. Of his three children, his son Robert took the greatest interest in telecommunication. The field continued to advance during Robert's upbringing, with innovations such as commercial radio broadcasting and television transmission tubes, for example. Telecommunication was already a booming field, so it was only natural that a young person would be interested in learning about it. Of course, it is highly plausible that J.O. inspired Robert to study electrical engineering at the Case School of Applied Science, now Case Western University. While in college, Robert spent summers working for the Ohio Northern Telephone Company, digging holes for the installation of telephone poles. Sadly, J.O. died while Robert was in college. Upon graduating, Robert soon found a job at North Electric Manufacturing Company, which was known for its telephone and switchboards. The company was based in a small town, Galion, Ohio, where, one could argue, this story really begins. There Robert and his high school sweetheart, MaryJane Avery, began their married life together.

Galion, with a population of 8,685, was where David Scott Campbell was born on September 23, 1941. Another birth in that year is certainly worth mentioning. While Campbell cooed in his bassinet, mathematician Claude Shannon began groundbreaking research on information transmission and how messages travel. His conclusions regarding the transactional nature of communication formed the basic framework for communication scholarship, known as information theory. In addition, in 1941 the Federal Communications Commission (FCC) released its watershed report on "Chain Broadcasting" to address monopolization of the airwaves.

It is very easy to "typecast" small American towns. To some, they all appear to be the same. Corner stores, farmland, a church, a school or two, and the homes of the residents are usually "given" elements. In his memoir, titled *I'm Just the Dad*, David Campbell reflects on his small-town surroundings with such a mindset:

> Galion, Ohio in the '40s and '50s had much the same effect
> on me as water has on fish. The area surrounds and affects,

nurtures too, but for the most part, young people just swim along from day to day bumping into the glass enclosure, not really minding it or being aware of the water.

In spite of this self-admitted deprecatory interpretation of his hometown, Campbell was very fond of his upbringing in Galion. He participated in the Boy Scouts, helped his parents with gardening and cooking, and enjoyed going on adventures with his friends. On one of these adventures, he received what he described as "a moniker that would follow me through school from the seventh grade on… 'Bugs.'" While being taught Morse code in the Boy Scouts, the instructor thought of this nickname, and for whatever reason, it stuck. Like most children of the 1940s, young Campbell enjoyed listening to the radio, including a diverse selection of programming. Some of these included the situational comedy "The Aldrich Family," the popular game show "Twenty Questions," as well as various political campaigns that made the airwaves in the '40s and 50s. In his memoir, Campbell recalls his recollections of listening to the radio during his upbringing:

> I can picture that large standing living room radio in my mind but there are no photographs. I can see in my mind all of us listening to one of Harry Truman's campaign speeches in 1948 when someone in the audience shouted, "Give 'em hell, Harry!"

Radio and telecommunication was a hot topic during Campbell's childhood. Just a few months after his twelfth birthday, physicists William Shockley, Calvin Fuller and Gerald Pearson invented the transistor. Watching this innovation take shape can certainly contribute to a fascination with electronics, as well as the content of the performances on the air.

As for many Americans, the "magic window" known as television soon entered the Campbell household. The nine-inch Garod set, which did not come with an antenna, would become a source of information and entertainment for the family. At various points, he helped his father make adjustments to the set, which involved the famous "test patterns" displayed on the screen. From the age of eight, Campbell watched popular children's programs such as "Howdy Doody," athletic programming, and political convention coverage. "We almost always watched the 'Huntley-Brinkley Report' on NBC," Campbell said, "[which was] a fifteen-minute news program that came on at 6:30 followed by some sort of variety program, a different one each night." Who would guess that he would later spend decades of his life teaching others about how to produce such programming?

Television was not the only visual medium from which Campbell found enjoyment. For Christmas one year, he was given a Dick Tracy camera, which was a point-and-shoot camera manufactured by Seymour Products. Due to its simple design, this was a perfect beginner camera, and it sparked a new passion in Campbell.

A forum for Campbell to develop both his photographic skills as well as writing abilities was his involvement with campus publications. As a senior, he served as a member of the newspaper and yearbook committees, which we can credit as the beginning of his skills in graphic design and layout. He would later teach graphics competencies in many college courses. This experience may also have been the precursor to Campbell's drive to provide his students with real-life learning experiences. The school newspaper, as described in the 1959 yearbook, provided a rigorous and realistic journalistic opportunity. "The Journalism Class served as reporters and not only reported school events, but also wrote many articles of interest." Campbell got to help edit a weekly page of the town's newspaper, The Galion Inquirer. These experiences undoubtedly contributed to his interest in journalism, graphic design, and eventually desktop publishing.

Galion was a great place for children to grow up: a small, close, and safe community. "All the time I lived there," said Campbell, "the back door was never locked and our cars sat in the driveway, keys in the ignition. Yes, burglars and car thieves existed then as now, we just felt secure." Secure in terms of offering kindness to strangers, too. In third grade, a new family moved into the community, and among them was a son named Charles Schultz. Campbell took it upon himself to welcome them to their new community. "He lived probably about seven blocks from me, and Galion is a small town, so it was in walking distance," recalls Schultz, who quickly became good friends with Campbell, or more appropriately, Bugs.

As Campbell grew up, his interests broadened greatly. Fortunately, Galion High School not only embraced his diverse hunger for knowledge but provided him with opportunities that would influence his life and career in more ways than one. "He was into everything a great deal," Schultz said. "He was a very active individual in our high school; he was well liked by everyone." Many teenagers will gain the attention of their fellow students through a specific niche they've carved out for themselves — such as being a football player or by challenging authority figures. Campbell's attention came largely through service and volunteerism. A regular churchgoer since childhood, he eventually joined the Christian leadership association, Hi-Y, participating for three years and ultimately becoming the vice president of the school's chapter. "He was vice president of Hi-Y; I was president of the Student Council," Schultz explained. "The Student Council and Hi-Y got together our senior year and we started a canned food drive for all the needy families around Galion at Christmas time." Campbell, Schultz, and classmate Jim Blosser not only organized the collection of these cans, but they also delivered them. "Bugs was very cognizant of needy families and trying to give back to the community. That was a big thrill for the three of us," Schultz said.

Throughout his high school years, he continued to satisfy his love for learning. He participated in science club, studied Latin for several semesters, and took drafting, where he was able to learn the skills of mechanical drawing. While he satisfied his curiosity in various areas of study, his long-time interest was the performing arts. Theatre and music played an important role in Campbell's life. From as early as first grade, he performed in plays and later became a member of the school choir. In physical education classes he was taught various forms of dance and would continue performing in various capacities throughout high school.

At Galion High School Campbell participated in multiple performance organizations such as the Glee Club, the Boys' Ensemble, as well as "The Keynotes," which was a boys' quartet. Singing alongside him was his buddy Chuck Schultz. "In high school, we were in three groups together: we were in the choir, we were in the Boy's Glee Club, and then Mr. Krichbaum, our choir director, selected four of us to be in a quartet." This group was called "The Keynotes" and was a source of pride and fun for Campbell. "I could not read a note of music, nor play the scale on the piano, but loved singing with a group," Campbell said. He received a lot of support from his family and much praise from the student body and was eventually named vice president of the choir.

Indirectly, Campbell's involvement in music would lead him into the next chapter of his life. "It was in my senior year that the quartet qualified to go to the Ohio finals in a singing competition which that year was held at Bowling Green State University," he said. "…I would later choose to apply to BGSU." Campbell's father also helped his son to develop public speaking skills through his involvement with the Kiwanis Club. On several occasions, Campbell appeared before the Galion chapter to deliver a reading, to discuss his experiences in the Boy Scouts, or to sing. Perhaps we can attribute these experiences to Campbell's interest in community involvement as a pedagogical strategy during his teaching career.

Just before graduating from Galion High School in 1959, Campbell would enter the classroom of Miriam Sayre, a speech and dramatics teacher. In addition, she was the play director for Galion High School and a highly regarded member of the community. "Her diction was as perfect as her posture," said Campbell. "Her stories of Galion were a treasure to hear from her lips. Her teaching was demanding in speech and English lit, relaxed and fun in dramatics." Schultz shares the same positive regard toward Sayre, as he too enrolled in her courses and acted in some of her performances at Galion.

> She was a gem. She was unusual for a high school drama teacher. We would probably do two if not three main stage shows, and a number of one-acts each year, which is an incredible active program in the late '50s in high school. And she was well known in the area.

Campbell acted in three plays during his senior year, as well as several during his sophomore and junior years at Galion. We can only assume that Ms. Sayre had a profound impact on Campbell, who declared Speech as his major at Bowling Green State University very soon afterward. Though he was leaving his small town, he would bring with him a vast palate of interests, talents, creative forms of self-expression, and a sense of pride in his upbringing. His interests were broad, but they all stemmed back to the nurturing and supportive environment that was provided by his school, his friends, and his family.

References
Bittner, J.R. (1985). *Broadcasting and Telecommunication: An Introduction*. Englewood Cliffs, New Jersey: Prentice-Hall.

Campbell, D.S. (n.d.). "Campbell Farms" [Unpublished family history.] (Undated, but presumably written after 2007.)

Campbell, D.S. (2001). *I'm just the Dad*. [Unpublished memoir.] Naples, Florida.

Dougherty, R. (1994). *Claude Shannon*. Retrieved June 5, 2018, from http://www.nyu.edu/pages/linguistics/courses/v610003/shan.html

Galion, Ohio Population 1940. (n.d.). Retrieved November 5, 2016, from http://worldpopulationreview.com/us-cities/galion-oh-population/

"J.O. Campbell, Expires After Long Illness" [Obituary]. Published in 1930, source unknown.

Schultz, C., & Schultz, P. Personal interview, March 12, 2018.

Snyder Funeral Homes. (2003). "Obituary for Miriam H. Sayre." Galion, Ohio. Retrieved March 16, 2018 from https://www.snyderfuneralhomes.com/obituary/miriam-h-sayre/

Reprinted From
Costa, J. T. (2018). *David Campbell: Story of a Career*. Morgantown, Pennsylvania: Masthof Press.

Interested in learning more about David Campbell?

Experience a career that is timelined by some of the most profound innovations in technology as well as the changing perception of "speech education" in academia. *David Campbell: Story of a Career* is the story of an educator who spent his career teaching students how to express themselves using media. All the while, Campbell was learning and growing as he embraced new opportunities, maintained resilience through setbacks, and succeeded in making a difference at his institution and, more importantly, in the lives of thousands of students.

Special features of this book include:
- Extensive interviews with family and friends
- Archived visuals and artifacts
- Additional segments from Campbell's original memoir
- Explanations of technological marvels from five different decades

David Campbell: Story of a Career
Written by Julian Costa
ISBN# 978-1601265975
Copyright © 2018
Masthof Press and Bookstore

Acknowledgements from David Campbell

I want to thank my dear friend and former colleague Michael Liberman who offered words of encouragement and gentle suggestions. Cindie Winters, a professional editor, made some editing changes then stopped, saying the work should be mine and in my own words. Cindie encouraged me from the start and was effusive with compliments. Lastly, my aunt Fran gave me correct spellings of family members' names and added details about my parents' lives in Norwalk, Ohio. Fran asked more than once, "How can you remember all of that?!"

David Scott Campbell

Naples, Florida
December, 2001